CHOSEN TO SERVE

THE LEGACY OF ALBERTA BRANNON
of Alberta's Tea Room

BARBARA DUFF-BRANNON

CHOSEN TO SERVE
Copyright © 2025 by BARBARA DUFF-BRANNON

ISBN: 979-8894791517 (sc)
ISBN: 979-8894791524 (e)

The Reading Glass Books
BOOKS

The Reading Glass Books
1-888-420-3050
www.readingglassbooks.com
production@readingglassbooks.com

TABLE OF CONTENT

FORWARD

Alberta Brannon, and her daughter-in-law, Barbara Brannon, shared many things in common, but, by far the most important, was their faith. That is why Barbara decided to write a book about her cherished MIL. "The book got in my spirit. I wanted to keep her legacy for the children and grandchildren. "Mother,' a mother to everyone, was known for her faith, her purpose and how she served," Barbara noted.

Alberta "served" by cooking and catering. Her food also tasted better with some "Amens" and she faithfully led a 6:00 a.m. morning prayer service at her church every week (Sunday-Friday) for 30 years. Alberta was given the opportunity to serve two United States presidents while they were in office: President John F. Kennedy and President George H. Bush. She also cooked for Civil Rights activist Rosa Parks, Actor James Earl Jones, and Actress Phyllis Diller. She served the greater Oklahoma City community, beginning her entrepreneurship at the Eastside Bakery, owned and operated by her husband James, in the late 1940's. Alberta's Tea Room opened in 1969. The restaurant was famous for Alberta's soulful buttered rolls, the best chicken salad, and fresh and flavorful apple pie with rum sauce. Chicken tetrazzini casserole, shrimp salad and her chocolate brownie with ice cream and chocolate fudge sauce.

Oklahomans loved Alberta's Rea Room, originally opened in the Discoveries Building on Grand Boulevard, and later moved to French Market Mall. It was the meeting place for many women's groups, a variety of clubs and friends who wanted to visit over lunch. Grandparents took their grandchildren for the wonderful desserts, and friends met for lunch after shopping. Birthdays and special occasions were celebrated with the Brannons' for years.

Alberta had many family members working in the Tea Room and son Chef Larry, husband of Barbara, still cooks these wonderful recipes in Oklahoma City to this day. Barbara noted that "Mother" was generous, happy, and laughed a lot. "She fed a lot of people. If someone was hungry, she fed them."

This is Barbara's second book. Her first book, ONE LIFE, MANY TESTIMONIES: A LEGACY OF GOD'S GRACE AND MERCY, was an example to young people, telling them how Barbara persevered in her life through many illnesses. As you read this book you will again see the same powerful God who manifested divinely for Barbara was the same God who also moved mightily for Alberta.

We are yet waiting for the Brannon Cookbook (Number 3 book by Barbara Brannon.)

Helen Ford Howe
Oklahoma Journalism Hall of Fame

Social writer for The Oklahoman
Newspaper, Oklahoma City, for over six decades.

DEDICATION

I dedicate this biography to my family "The Brannons" in honor of my Mother-In-Law, Alberta Brannon who was our rock and inspiration.

To all our friends who submitted a favorite memory of Alberta Brannon and Alberta's Tea Room

I love you,

Barbara

ACKNOWLEDGMENTS

Thank you, Father, thank you, Jesus, thank you, Holy Ghost. To God be the glory for the things He has done in my life. The writing of this book has been in my heart for several years. 2024 I knew I had to get started. It was harder than I thought especially since I had already written and published my first book. I asked for help and thanked God I received what I needed.

Secondly, I thank my amazing, patient, kind and so much more husband, Larry Brannon, for again giving me the space and time to work on my project. Most of the time late at night.

I want to thank those who submitted what I called "A Favorite Memory" of you and Alberta or your time at the Alberta's Tea Room. The love I received with this project has been insurmountable.

Mrs. Helen Ford Howe was so excited to write the Forward for this book. Thank you for being a loving friend and part of our family.

Special thanks to my son David, who read my manuscript with strong detective eyes and great criticism that made me dig deeper to include more facts. He suggested I needed more eyes looking at the project. I asked Dr. Elicia Brannon-Little, my niece, Wilma Brannon, my sister-in-love, and my daughter Carla. These ladies also gave my project the help it needed. I cannot thank you all enough.

Finally, I want to thank Amanda Brown, Senior Acquisition Editor from Reading Glass Books publishing company for contacting me concerning my first book, One Life, Many Testimonies: A Legacy of God's Grace and Mercy. I shared with her that I was writing my second book, and she was excited to offer her expertise. I received a team, Trixie Evans, publishing services Associate, Raquel Martinez, event specialist and more. Thank you all for the help to bring this biography to life and fruition.

I pray God's blessings over you all.

Thank you,

Barbara Duff-Brannon

PART I

"THE BEGINNING OF ALBERTA'S STORY"

"I CAN DO ALL THINGS THROUGH CHRIST WHICH STRENGTHENETH ME."
PHILIPPIANS 4:13

Alberta Susong-Brannon was an entrepreneur, a spiritual and religious woman, faithful, loving, hardworking, a woman of God, and so much more. To understand her life and legacy, let us journey back to her beginning. Born to Roy and Ola Susong in Clinton, Oklahoma on August 19, 1920, Alberta was welcomed by her older sister, Ethel Catherine Blanch Susong. These sisters became an inseparable pair, answering the nicknames Snook (Ethel) and Tomp (Alberta), which stuck with them for life. The love they shared for each other was truly amazing; when you saw one, you saw the other.

Alberta was a smart child who excelled in her studies, especially in math and reading, within the Clinton, Oklahoma public school system. She had an excellent attendance record, not missing a single day from first grade until her final day of the ninth grade.

When Alberta met the tall, handsome, light-skinned baseball player named James Leon Brannon, with his black wavy hair, it was love at first sight. James Leon could not keep his eyes off Alberta either; her big brown eyes, long black hair, and hourglass figure captivated him. Their love continued to grow, even though James Leon was eight years older than Alberta, who was sixteen at the time. He was traveling with a local Negro Baseball League and despite the distance, they found time for each other and were married in March 1936.

Their first child, James Jr., was born that same year in December. Three years later, after their move to Weatherford, Oklahoma, their second son, Roy Lee, was born in December 1939. James Leon loved playing baseball but had to quit the team because Alberta needed him at home since their family was growing and the Baseball League was not providing sufficient financial support.

They moved again, this time to Oklahoma City, where Leon, as Alberta lovingly called him, could find a better job. In June 1942, they welcomed another son, whom they named Bobby Ray. A couple of years later, Alberta found herself pregnant again, and another son was born. Marvin Eugene arrived in April 1945. The Brannon household was filled with boys. Alberta had her hands full, even though she had asked her mother, Ola, how she managed to have only two children. Her mother replied that she prayed and asked God for two girls, and that was exactly what she got. Alberta jokingly asked her mother, "So why did God let me have all these boys?" even though she loved every one of them. Her sister Ethel was always there, smiling and helping take care of those boys.

Before she knew it, Alberta was pregnant again, but to her surprise and dismay, the pregnancy ended in a miscarriage. Difficult as it was to lose that child, Alberta had to be strong. It was not long before the Lord blessed her, and she conceived again, delivering a beautiful baby girl in January 1946. They named the precious little girl Alberta Darlene. Alberta's best friend, Elizabeth Rhynehart, could not believe the news: "It's a girl!" Knowing that all her previous children were boys, they were all so excited. Ethel was overjoyed. She now had a cute little niece to dress up in fancy dress and put ribbons in her hair.

Although Alberta was incredibly happy and excited to have a baby girl among four very rambunctious boys, her childbearing days were not over. In January 1949, Alberta delivered another baby boy. They named him Harold Lynn. Eighteen months later, in June 1950, their sixth son was born. They named him Larry Franklin, but everyone called him Joe. To their happiness and surprise, Larry was the last child born into this family. Alberta said, "The Lord was happy with what He had given her and closed up her womb." They now have six sons and one daughter. They lived in Carver Dale housing addition on the east side of Oklahoma City in two bedrooms one-bathroom single family home.

Darlene would often wonder if the baby her mother lost was her big sister. Being the only girl, she had to be tough, but she learned how to manage her brothers! Darlene's baby brother Larry, asked her "where did she sleep since all the brothers were in one room?" He did not know until he was grown that she slept at the foot of their parent's bed on a cot.

Suffering for years with her eyes, Alberta's sister Ethel, at just twenty-four years old, lost her eyesight after surgery to remove cataracts from both eyes. That did not stop the courageous woman. Learning how to live with her blindness for years with confidence in herself, Ethel decided to move to Los Angeles, CA, where she could be on her own. She found an apartment and gained employment. Yes, she was blind, but very independent. She had her own special way of counting money and cooking. She loves to go shopping and would call anyone that did not mind taking her. Years later she moved to Chicago to experience life in the windy city. She enjoyed a short stint singing backup vocals for the Great Mahaila Jackson. After being away from home for years, Ethel received news that her mother was terribly ill, and she decided to return home to help with her care. In 1962, After a lengthy illness, Alberta and Ethel's mother Ola Susong passed away.

In search of a better job to support his family, James Leon began working at Brown's Bakery in Uptown, OKC. After working several years at Brown's and learning the trade of a baker, in the late '40s, Leon and Alberta opened The Eastside Bakery on North Bath Avenue in Oklahoma City, OK. That was the beginning of a long history in the food service. James

Jr. gave the rendition of being tasked with rising early to help with making donuts at the bakery before going to school in the mornings. The bakery business was doing well until the shop caught fire and burned down. James and Alberta were saddened but not defeated. They were raising their children to be strong and willing to work hard to accomplish their goals in life. James went back to Brown's Bakery, working part-time during the night shift and as a chauffeur for Mr. R.D. Cravens during the day.

Alberta and Ethel Susong

James Leon Brannon, Sr.

Catherine Willson Alberta's
Grandmother

Alberta Brannon/Ethel Susong

Alberta and James Brannon

Alberta receives Award

Alberta and James at
Eastside Bakery

PART II

"COOKING AND CATERING"

"LET THE FAVOR OF THE LORD OUR GOD BE UPON US AND ESTABLISH THE WORK OF OUR HANDS UPON US; YES, ESTABLISH THE WORK OF OUR HANDS."
PSALM 90: 17

Alberta always loved to cook, and upon getting acquainted with one of Oklahoma City's leading black cooks and caterers, Laura McMurry, Alberta begun her first catering job in 1950 when her baby Larry was just six months old. Alberta learned a lot working side by side with Ms. McMurry, but it proved to be both challenging and rewarding.

During her years serving under Ms. McMurry, Alberta had the privilege of training other young people in the catering business, including one young lady particularly, Mary Evelyn Clark, her oldest son James Jr's wife. Mary Clark had been raised in the Oklahoma countryside and knew a bit about cooking. She was an adaptive learner, and soon they became a team. Mary, May as the family lovingly called her, helped Alberta for many years with catering, as a waitress, and as a cake baker too.

In 1955 Alberta and husband James Leon moved their family from Carver Dale to Euclid Ave. into a three-bedroom one bathroom home. This gave their only daughter Darlene, her own room. Alberta always said, "every move has been better."

After many years of service, Ms. McMurry's health began to decline, and she was no longer able to serve her clients. Alberta, who loved the work, enlisted her family and friends to help with large parties. It was not long before Alberta started her own catering business from her home on Euclid Ave.

Alberta's youngest son Larry often talked about his mother catering from their home. They learned how to peel, devein and clean shrimp outside in the backyard for many parties. Larry said he, Darlene and Harold had orders from their mother when she left to go on a catering party saying "I want this kitchen cleaned before I get home. Harold told me he had to sweep, mop and clean all around the stove and oven. Larry would laugh when he told me Darlene was the fastest dishwasher, but they had to take turns. That kitchen had to be spotless.

Alberta expected excellence in all that she did to serve her clients. After 14 years of catering from her home, Alberta's name had become a favorite and was well-known in Nichols Hills, Quail Creek, and Crown Heights.

Alberta catered for Senator Robert S. Kerr and his family on many occasions and received the honor of her life in October of 1961. Alberta was offered the opportunity of catering several meals for Senator Robert S. Kerr while hosting the President of the United States, John F. Kennedy. President Kennedy had come to Big Cedar, OK to dedicate US Highway 259. After the highway dedication, President Kennedy and Senator Kerr returned to the ranch where some of Senator Kerrs prized cattle were displayed in a private showing.

Alberta's second son, Roy Lee Brannon, was attending Oklahoma University in Norman, OK, studying to become an architect when his mother received the offer to cook for the President of the United States for the weekend. Roy was happy and very excited to help his mother with this catering endeavor.

Alberta had to undergo a series of physical examinations and background checks, as did those chosen to help her cook and serve at the ranch in Poteau. That was the most elaborate dinner of her life. Photos and news reports went around the world featuring Alberta Brannon with President John F. Kennedy and her son Roy Lee Brannon along with Tito Bono, Senator Kerr's Butler.

Since catering for Oklahoma State Senator Robert S. Kerr and President John F. Kennedy, Alberta was also given the privilege to cater for other celebrities such as Vincent Price, Danny Thomas, and comedian Phyllis Diller.

"My children, born 1969, 1973, 1976, grew up having lunch at Alberta's Tea Room at least once a week. Their grandparents made sure that they did not miss the excellent chicken salad, the best hot apple pie in the world and always the brownies, ice cream and hot fudge sauce prepared with love by the Brannon family. The rest of us loved the homemade rolls, the chicken tetrazzini, and the fruit salad with special dressing. The same recipes today, cooked by Chef Larry Brannon, reminds us of home, and the "good ole days." We started our love of Alberta Brannon's cooking at Discoveries, at NW 63rd and Grand, and then at the Tea Room at French Market Mall.

The Brannon family is such a blessing. None of them ever met a stranger. Hospitality has been on their minds for decades. They oversaw a community, favorite restaurant for 25 years and then opened Brannon Catering until this day. The number one place for our club meetings during the years 1969 – 1998 was Alberta's.

Many of the family members and in-laws (Barbara that I know of) were part of the extended hospitality the Tea Room offered, and some family members are still active today with Chef Larry Brannon. All have a great devotion to food service! They still prepare holiday dinners for us and cook up the best turkey and dressing and beef tenderloin in town… plus the famous apple pie with rum sauce, and all the other very special dishes that people in Oklahoma City cherish and love! Thanks for the memories."

-Helen Ford Howe

"I am so grateful for the privilege I had to be able to work for Mother Alberta Brannon, at Alberta's Tea Room. I remember her coming to pick me up along with a few other Mother's and taking us to Morning Prayer at Page Sanctuary Church before

we went to work. She was a prayer worrier and faithful Woman of God.

I remember I had gone to our National Women's Convention and upon my return home I told Mother Alberta, I just do not feel good. Her reply was "you are probably pregnant." I said NO I do not think so. Again, she stated go to the Doctor. I went to the Dr., and he said you are pregnant. I will never forget that we had a good laugh; that was funny."
-District Missionary Barbara M. Jackson

"I remember in 1959 Alberta helped Ms. MacMurry with my wedding 65 years ago. I also remember the Birthday parties, wedding showers she served for our family. I remember the first Alberta's Tea Room in the Discoveries building. The banana cream pie was our favorite. We still order it on Holidays."
-Janice Segell

"What a remarkable woman Sister Alberta Brannon was. I came to Oklahoma City in 1972, I was introduced to her by Sister LeOra Hodge. Sister Alberta was such an inspiration in my life, she taught me how to pray at the age of 20, every morning Monday through Friday rain or shine ice or snow on the ground she would pick me up and take me to 6:00 prayer which at that time was being held at Page Sanctuary Church of God in Christ 212 North Byers. This was one of her assignments given to her by God, down through the 30 years she was there many people came in for prayer from all over Oklahoma City and beyond. I have so many fond memories of Sister Alberta Brannon. She had so much wisdom she was lovable, caring, giving, peaceful and she had a sense of humor."
-Dinna Coleman

"I'm the "Doctor" and Grandma Bert and Pops were my patients. She let me drive her station wagon to the store and I always kept it nice and cleaned out. I did a lot of things for her when the Tea Room was open. I remember when Pops had a Maroon Lincoln. I kept it nice and clean, but he would not let me or anyone else drive it."

"I loved Grandma & Grandpa. I used to spend the night at their house sometime. We would go out and do some shopping and whatever."

"I would cut their yard, and Grandma Bert, told me I was the best worker at the Tea Room and best yard cutter ever. I went to California with them once and we had a really good time. I miss them so much, but I know they are in a better place."

-Stevie Brannon

"As an adult, mom said, "Every move that we made was better." Our first home was in the Carverdale Addition, just north of Douglas High School, off NE 10th street. We lived in a very modest home; nice but very modest. That home had only two bedrooms and one bathroom. The bathroom did not have a shower, so we all had to take baths, wash the tub and get out as quick as possible.

There were nine of us; six boys and one girl, and mom and dad. I did not find out until we were grown where my sister slept. The six boys slept in one bedroom and my sister said that she slept in a cot at the foot of our parent's bed in their bedroom.

If we were poor, I did not know it because we always had food and unity at home. My mom and dad were both hard workers and they taught us how to work. My dad was a baker working at different bakeries; he also had a job as a driver for a family, as well as assisting my mother in later years with her catering business.

At five years old we moved to another home at 1125 E. Euclid and that is when my mom began to get into catering with Laura McMurry. After Ms. McMurry retired, mother expanded her catering business with new clients, and we started helping mom at home to prepare food as well.

From an early age I saw that things were not always easy and even during her busy schedule she taught us to have faith in God and to love everyone. She taught me how near God is to us. She would say, "He is as close as your breath" and that gave me something to hold on to.

Life brought many challenges, but on one evening when I was in grade school, we saw how mom's faith in God gave us a great victory. My brother Marvin was driving by himself and the police began to follow him but they did not have their front lights turned on and initially he did not know it was the police that were following him. Since he was not sure who was behind him or why they were following him, he began to try to outrun them and go home. He drove home and when he did the police arrested him for speeding.

Mr. Jimmy Stewart, an advocate for blacks in the community, spoke up for Marvin saying that he was a good kid from a good family. The police still arrested Marvin and took him downtown to jail. Mother found out that his bond was $300.00. She did not have the money so she called different friends and neighbors and was able to raise the $300.00. My mom called an older woman that was a prayer partner and they prayed and she advised mom to continue praying and be still when she went to court the next morning. Marvin was not physically hurt and did not have to spend the night in jail.

Mom went to court and prayed quietly while sitting and listening. The police officers had conflicting stories and false evidence; the judge then threw the case out and gave mom the $300.00 back that she had paid the night before for Marvin's bail bond.

Before we knew about Martha Stewart, Jacques Pepin, or Paul Prudhomme of Louisiana, Mother taught us the art of fine dining; from setting the table, to serving properly from the right side. Now you purchase shrimp already peeled and cleaned, but we learned how to clean the vein out of the back of the shrimp in our backyard.

From helping my mom as a child, I began to take interest in food service as well. I was so amazed to see how my mom would cook for so many people just simply from her home kitchen. One time she was asked to cook and serve food to a group of students at Spring Lake Amusement Park on Eastern Ave (Martin Luther King Ave.) and Spring Lake Dr. When she arrived at the Amusement park ready to serve the lunch, she was refused entrance into the park because she was black and was redirected to the public park across the street.

After segregation and restaurants in OKC begin to be open to blacks. My mom and dad enjoyed going to the Mexican restaurant, Casa Bonita on 39th Expressway and Portland Ave.

Later, Mom had the opportunity to cater at the Oklahoma Art Museum located at the State Fair Grounds, and the Boomerang, an annual Golf Tournament, catering dinners at private homes for clients in Nichols Hills. One of the largest events that we catered from Alberta's Tea Room was for 1200 people at the Oklahoma National Cowboy and Western Museum (formerly called the Cowboy Hall of Fame).

Some of mom's personal favorites items to make were the orange Jell-O molds made with mandarin oranges, the tomato aspic, and the homemade fruit dressing.

People do not know that many mornings after morning prayer mom would pick me up for work and on the way, we would stop by Jim's Grocery at 63rd and Kelley and get Honey Buns for breakfast before going to the Tea Room.

Mom's faith, determination, and integrity is what after all these years, I continue to hold on to."

- Chef Larry F. Brannon, Sr.

Alberta with President John F. Kennedy in Poteau, Ok. With Tito Bono and her son, Roy Brannon.

Alberta with daughters in Hawaii

A family affair at Alberta's Tea Room in the Discoveries building.

Alberta and friends
Cinderella and Gladys

James, Alberta, and Uncle Dudley Wilson

Darlene, Alberta and Larry

Darlene and a few waitresses in
front of Alberta's Tea Room at
Discoveries building

James, Alberta, Barbara and Larry Brannon at wedding reception.

PART III

"ALBERTA'S FAITH IN GOD"

"I WAS GLAD WHEN THEY SAID UNTO ME, LET US GO INTO THE HOUSE OF THE LORD."
PSALM 122:1

Alberta's day started incredibly early. Six days a week, she led a 6:30 morning prayer at Page Sanctuary Church for thirty years. Along with her sister Ethel, LeOra Hodge, Cordelia Allen, Jean Jones, Maydell Hurd, Fannie Dickens, and other members of the church, who collectively witnessed God performing miracles after pray request were made.

Alberta's passion for cooking was second only to her passion for serving the Lord, Jesus Christ. She loved God's people and did everything in her power to help everyone she could, whether it was hiring them to work in her catering business, giving them money, paying their bills, buying shoes for their children, or even paying college tuition. Alberta allowed God to use her to bless people. She put her faith to work, praying for those who were sick and needed God's help and salvation. I will always remember Mother Alberta praying "Lord you know." "We pray your blessings over your people here there and everywhere." Before my husband Larry and I were married he told me he believed that if I could get to the morning prayer with his mother and A-nee, I would be healed. I was young but I believed Larry and I trusted God. Mother Alberta prayed for me and with me many times. I am healed today after suffering for twenty-four years with an incurable disease called Myasthenia Gravis.

Her faith was tested when she was diagnosed with a cancerous tumor during a required physical exam before cooking and serving President Kennedy. The doctor wanted to remove the tumor, but she refused surgery, choosing instead to pray and wait for God to heal her. She suffered for eighteen months without telling anyone, not even her husband or children, and never returned to the doctor. She had no treatment and took no medicine. Alberta held on to her faith and trusted in God, enduring serious pain and weakness from the tumor in her body. One morning, lying in bed talking to God and pondering how to tell her children and husband, she said that God spoke to her and asked her, "Do you expect to get better or get worse, live or die?" She said she then jumped out of bed and shouted, "I expect to get better, I expect to live!" She went to the bathroom, and the tumor drained out of her body into the toilet basin. She praised Almighty God for healing her body and shared her experience with her husband James Leon.

Mother Alberta would often quote 2 Timothy 2:7 "For God has not given us the spirit of fear; but of power, and of love, and of a sound mind."

She shared her testimony often to build others' faith and encourage them to trust God as a healer and deliverer. That was not the only time she experienced God's miraculous healing. Alberta's daughter Darlene had boiled a pot of water to mop the floor and poured it into a mop bucket. Her 2-year-old son Ken ran through the kitchen, slipped and accidentally fell into the hot bucket of water, scalding his back. Darlene screamed and grabbed her baby and rushed him over to her mother Alberta's house, knowing she would pray and know what to do. Alberta took the baby and immediately began praying and poured blessed oil all over his body. The baby went to sleep, and the next day he was up and running around like nothing had happened. That was truly a blessing and miracle from God. He did not have any further infections or negative reactions from the incident.

There are so many stories of Alberta's faith and trust in Jesus Christ that have blessed our family through the years. Alberta did not and would not go to the dentist, no matter how severe her toothache was or how long she took all her problems to the Lord in prayer. Before we knew it, she had a tooth in her hand saying, "look, God has delivered me" right there on the altar at Page Sanctuary Church. Wow, that was an amazing testimony.

If someone misplaced their belongings or anything Alberta would say, "there is nothing lost in God's kingdom" she would repeat that until the person let her know that what was lost had been found. She had great faith. I was told about a neighbor that would bleed from cancer after surgery. Alberta would go over to her house and pray and read the scripture, Ezekiel 16:6-8 "When I passed by thee, and saw thee polluted in thine own blood, I said unto thee when thou were in, thou blood, Live. She said the woman's bleeding would stop.

A couple other quotes were "Lord keep on speaking to us through your word" and "Lord thank you for persevering our homes and the homes of your people everywhere." She taught us how to wait and have faith in God as we prayed.

Alberta prayed and waited and was excited to move again when she found her dream home, a white brick ranch with a two-car garage, three bedrooms, two bathrooms and a large backyard and a unique orange colored front door. Her children had a custom brick mailbox installed at the front curb to accompany the property and added a cement driveway with an extended parking area for all the family cars. Mother and Pop's house was the place to be on Sundays after church. Pops had fried chicken, okra, creamed corn, cornbread, and peach cobbler prepared for all their family.

After the experience of catering for the President, Mrs. LaMone Kerr, the wife of Senator Robert S. Kerr, and her family encouraged Alberta to move forward in her career and open a restaurant. After earnestly praying the Lord to ensure this was His Will, she received an answer of "YES." In the spring of 1969, with the financial support of the Kerr family, a new restaurant called Alberta's Tea Room opened in the DISCOVERIES Inc. building located on NW Grand Blvd. in Oklahoma City, OK.

This was truly a family business: Alberta Brannon as the owner, Roy Lee Brannon was the general manager, James L. Brannon Jr. was the head chef, James Leon Brannon was the pastry chef, and Larry Franklin Brannon as the executive catering chef. Alberta's staff also included sister Ethel, their daughter Darlene, daughters-in-law, grandchildren, and friends.

Alberta's Tea Room began as a place for ladies' luncheons, being open only for lunch initially, but it soon became the go-to venue for weddings, birthdays, anniversaries, Easter, Mother's Day, and all sorts of occasions. Big companies often hold their business meetings there. The family prided themselves on everything being homemade, from the sandwich bread and buns to the cakes, pies, and soups. The restaurant was beautiful and spacious, and there was no other Black-owned establishment like it in Oklahoma.

"Growing up in Kansas City, I would like to come to Oklahoma City to visit my Aunt May Singer. We always went to Alberta's Tea Room for a special aunt/niece lunch. In 1973 I moved to Oklahoma City, which gave me more opportunities to regularly go to Alberta's Tea Room.

The best tetrazzini ever, best fruit salads, unique special lettuce salads and the best delicious pastries in our community.

So, I must say that Alberta's Tea Room was owned by a wonderful family, raising above ordinary restaurant establishments and providing white starched tablecloths and service in such a gentil environment all wrapped up with dignity."
-Mrs. Hedra Merson

"One of the many wonderful memories I have of Bert is when Mary, Darlene and I went with her to Hawaii. Pops may have been with us I cannot recall. We really enjoyed the adventure and experiencing the beautiful sights.

Us younger ladies had a time just keeping up with Bert. We Island hopped in planes that we were not sure would stay up in the air and scared us a bit, but Bert just prayed as usual and knew it would be OK. We had a great time!!!"

-Hattie Harris

"As a young girl, going to Alberta's Tea room was always a very special treat. The food was DELICIOUS, and we insisted our children use their very best manners.

The highlight of my family memories was having my mother, Edna's 75 Birthday party at the Tea Room. It was a beautiful party with LeRoy, James, Larry, and Alberta, making everyone feel welcome. Our guests were excited to share a lovely dinner to celebrate Mother.

We all loved the Chicken Tetrazzini, hot rolls, with Lemon & Chocolate Tarts for dessert. Did U forget the Chicken Salad we always had for lunch?

It is a joy to recall our three generations that loved going to Alberta's Tea Room. She was Oklahoma's BEST!!!"

-Nancy Ellis

"My grandma was a praying woman (her and my great Aunt Nanny). She went to prayer every morning, I believe around 6:00 a.m. She would pray in the Tea Room throughout the day, often quoting a scripture. Seeing her prayer all the time instilled some of the same values in me. I know God was always there listening and guiding her steps. She was a prayer warrior. I know the whole family was blessed because she always kept the faith.

I remember when Grandma Bert would feed this homeless man who would knock on the back door of the Tea Room. Uncle Roy tried to run him off, but grandma would go and get a full plate of food and give it to him as if she were serving a paying customer.

The Tea Room served the best gourmet food I have ever tasted in my life. So, I know why the homeless man continued to come back. My grandma told me, if someone is hungry, she is going to feed them. She always mailed a check to Feed the Children because she believed in not letting anyone go hungry. She told me if someone asks for food, let them eat, which is exactly what the Bible says.

I never saw my grandma upset or being argumentative. Sometimes when I walked in the kitchen at the Tea Room late, she said she is going to count to 10. She would hold her hands in the air and one finger at a time, she would count to 10. Then she took a deep breath and said "okay" and continued like nothing ever happened. It is funny because I think of her counting to 10 and often use it as an example when I teach about Emotional Intelligence. Additionally, if I get frustrated, I take a few seconds to count to 10 then I try to move on as my grandma did.

Grandma believed in working. She was a hard worker. Because of her work ethic, my dad is a hard worker, and I am a hard worker. If the Tea Room doors were open, she was there. I do not recall her ever being sick at the Tea Room. I cannot recall the last time I called in sick to take off at any of my jobs. There were times when I was not feeling well but I did not believe I needed to call in. I realized that most of the time, I felt better after going to work rather than lying in bed all day. The Tea Room was full of laughter, fun, and family. My grandma taught me to work, keep moving forward, and make the most of each day."

- Dr. Elicia Brannon Little

"While my memories of Bert were busy parties in Alberta's Tea Room. Often, there would be parties or a catering job. These jobs were sudden and not recorded in the reservation book. In moments like these, Bert was very calm and patient. Most likely praying, while preparing food at the last minute. During opening hours, Bert operated the cash register. (The cash register does not operate

like cash registers do now.) In fact, it did not add, subtract, or give the correct amount of change. Bert would simply do the math inside her head. She was always correct.

Once the lunch hour was over, and cleanup was complete, I remember on many days Bert and Jean (a co-worker) looking through quilt pattern books. In moments like these, after selecting a pattern, Bert and Jean would begin. Simply by planning, arranging, and sewing quilts for her family. In fact, we still have ours!"

– Karlette Brannon

"Grandma Bert was more than just the heart of our family; she was our anchor, our guiding light, and our constant source of love and strength.

She poured her soul into everything she did, especially into Alberta's Tea Room. That restaurant was not just a place to eat—it was a second home. It was where I worked during school breaks and during the summer with my cousins. The Tea Room was a place where generations came together, working side by side under her gentle leadership. Her food fed the body, but her love, faith, and warmth fed the soul.

She was a woman of deep faith, a grandmother who prayed every single day. Her prayers wrapped around us like a protective blanket, unseen but always felt. In her quiet moments, she spoke to God not just for herself, but for all of us—lifting up our names, our worries, and our dreams.

What made Grandma Bert so special was not just what she did—it was who she was. She was kind, strong, and extremely generous. She showed us what it meant to work hard, to care deeply, and to always make room in her Ford Crown Victoria station wagon for one more grandkid."

-David Brannon

6:00 AM Prayer with a few of the prayer team members

James and Alberta's 48th Wedding Anniversary celebration at the Fairmont Hotel in Dallas, TX

James and Alberta at International Women's Convention

PART IV

"NEW LOCATION IN FRENCH MARKET MALL"

"THE LORD HATH APPEARED OF OLD UNTO ME, SAYING, YEA, I HAVE LOVED THEE WITH AN EVERLASTING LOVE: THEREFORE, WITH LOVINGKINDNESS HAVE I DRAWN THEE."
JEREMIAH 31:3

In 1980, the family received an offer to move into a new space on the second level of the French Market Mall, located at the corner of NW 63rd & May Avenue. At the new location, Alberta's Tea Room occupied a nine-thousand-square-foot space divided into three dining rooms, a kitchen, and an office. The Tea Room was the largest space for everyday walk-in lunches. The Garden Club Room was mostly used for small private luncheons, and the Green Room for business meetings.

When business was a bit slow, mostly due to harsh weather, Alberta, quite the quilter, would be busy with needles, thread, and fabric spread out on the table. Alberta stitched an amazing amount of beautiful handmade quilts for various friends and family members. She made sure all her grandchildren had one of her quilts to remember her by.

The Brannon family loved to celebrate Mother and Pop's wedding anniversary in March. It had to be planned as not to be on any dates that were booked in the Tea Room. We would all drive down to Dallas, Texas one weekend and stay at the beautiful Anatole Hotel or the prestigious Fairmont Hotel. It was always an exciting weekend with their children and grandchildren. It was a nice time to enjoy the brothers and sisters' nieces and nephews and all the cousins to get to play with each other. The Buffet was so fabulous and delicious.

In March 1986, Alberta and James Leon celebrated their 50th wedding anniversary with a three-day celebration. Friday evening with a fabulously catered dinner party by Carol and Jerry Taylor for all six sons, one daughter, and their spouses at the home of their youngest son Larry and his wife

Barbara. Saturday at noon, there was an elegant luncheon served in the Tea Room with their children, grandchildren, great-grandchildren, family, and a few friends. Sunday was the big Wedding Anniversary reception after the two renewed their vows with family and friends looking on held at the spacious, fabulously decorated Alberta's Tea Room. This affair was open to all her clients and customers. It was a beautiful, touching, uplifting celebration of love and commitment. Marvin Eugene made the beautiful white, seven-tier wedding cake of assorted flavors. It was spectacular! Breathtakingly beautiful floral arrangements adorned each table in the room. Family friend Ms. Agnes Gordon and her catering company helped serve, and the food was, as always, delicious.

Alberta wore a beautiful white Lily Ann long-sleeved dress that fastened down the front with white round flat buttons, accompanied by purple and white corsage. She stepped out in a pair of white leather J. Renee heels. James Leon was dressed in a black tuxedo, white shirt, black bow tie, and a matching boutonniere. This couple epitomized the love that God instructed us to have for one another and to love our neighbors as we love ourselves. They taught us how to love, respect, have faith, be responsible, take pride in all we do, hold on to each other in marriage, and never forget to pray and trust God in everything we do.

Through the years, James and Alberta were a team. They would travel to California on vacation every year during the summer to visit family and friends, always with children and grandchildren in tow. I remember one year me; Larry and our family were able to take Mother and Pops on their vacation in a rented RV that carried seven of us. That was so much fun, to be able to have space and move around while rolling down the highway. In San Francisco, Pops, would go to the San Francisco Giant's baseball game and our boys Larry II and David got to go with their grandpa, to Candlestick Park for the first time. Pops loved the games. I went shopping with

Mother Alberta with her ole school friends. We later traveled down to Los Angeles to visit Alberta's uncles and aunts. We took the children out to the Pacific Ocean Park, a nautical-themed amusement park they also loved the beach.

Alberta also convinced her husband to accompany her to the International Women's Convention on a few occasions, held in different states across the United States. They enjoyed this time worshipping God and hearing good Bible teaching. They also took a trip to Hawaii with their daughter Darlene and two daughters-in-law Mary and Hattie.

In April 1987, the Brannon family was brought to heartbreaking sadness with the passing of Alberta and James's third son, Bobby Ray Brannon. Bobby followed in his dad's footsteps becoming a baker. He loved working at the bakery. This was a great loss because Uncle Bobby was the laughter, fun, and joy of every family gathering. Even during his sickness, Bobby would have everyone laughing. We miss him even now.

A year after saying goodbye to our brother Bobby Ray, James Leon Brannon, or "Pops" as his children called him, the head pastry chef of Alberta's Tea Room, passed away in 1988, two years after they celebrated fifty years of marriage. The strong woman that Alberta was, she continued to serve and be a witness of God's mighty power, even while grieving. Chef James Jr. and Chef Larry stepped up and continued baking the family's famous apple pie with rum sauce and those mouth-watering yeast rolls. Pops taught them well and his legacy lived on.

In 1990, President George H. Bush visited Oklahoma City, and the Daily Oklahoman for an event catered and served by Alberta's Tea Room. Alberta was blessed to be honored with the privilege of serving another President of the United States.

News 5 anchor B.J. Glover and Anthony Foster came out to Alberta's Tea Room to interview Alberta Brannon and the family for a special show on Black-owned businesses in

Oklahoma. B.J. Glover enjoyed the Chicken Tetrazzini while Anthony Foster dined on the Chicken Salad. When dessert was served, Foster was given the opportunity to sample a slice of homemade hot apple pie with rum sauce made by Chef James Jr. He could hardly wait to conclude the interview so he could eat that slice of pie. "Wow! This is amazing," he said.

In September 1995, Alberta's sister, Ethel, suffered a major stroke that left her unable to walk or talk. Ethel was Alberta's morning prayer partner, dishwasher at the Tea Room, best friend, and all-around helper. They did everything together, and everything began to change at the Tea Room without "Auntie," pronounced (A-nee) as the children lovingly called her. Although Ethel was not physically able to talk or work anymore, we learned how to communicate with her. She loved dressing up and going to church on Sunday mornings to praise and worship the Lord. That did not change or stop because she loved the Lord. We took great care of her at home, doting on her every need.

Around 1996, businesses began to suffer as the French Market Mall started losing tenants due to an increase in their lease agreement. This was a great concern for the Tea Room as well, but that never stopped Alberta from cooking and serving the best food possible to keep her clients coming.

God blessed Alberta and her family with the opportunities to cater and serve notable figures, such as Civil Rights Activist Rosa Parks, who was the guest speaker for the National Forum for Black Public Administrators Sooner Chapter (NFBPA) Pathway to Freedom Tour '96 Luncheon held on July 18, 1996, at Alberta's Tea Room. This event was another great experience for the people of Oklahoma, especially the Black community.

On Mother's Day, May 1997, our families were planning to gather for dinner at our home when Alberta fell on the back porch steps. It was a serious fall, and we were unable to lift her up because she was in server pain the paramedics were called. We spent the rest of the day at the hospital. After x-rays were taken, it was revealed that Alberta's right hip was broken. Because Alberta was not a person to take medicine, the medical team had trouble getting her sedated. We later learned that Alberta had suffered a stroke that caused her to fall and break her hip. This marked the beginning of a long road and many changes in Alberta and our family.

———————————

"What lovely memories I have of going to Alberta's Tea Room, the atmosphere was so beautiful and inviting. The food was always delicious, especially the Chicken Salad and that fabulous Hot Apple Pie with Rum Sauce. I cannot forget those Hot Rolls. I'm getting hungry now just thinking about it.

I always enjoyed getting to know the family and all those grandchildren."

-Ms. Shirley Blaik

"Grandma Bert always inspired me to put my best foot forward, always encouraging me to do better and be better. I appreciated her thoughtful insights and her willingness to always listen. One of her many sayings (and she had many) that I will always remember is that if we wanted to do something or achieve something she would say "if the Lord says the same, it will happen". This quote has stuck with me throughout my entire life and has helped me through difficult times. Grandma Bert had a quick wit and a great sense of humor in addition to an excellent example a strong Black woman who loved and protected her family unconditionally. She was truly the foundation of the Brannon family."

-Roy L. Brannon Jr.

Chatting with Ms. D'Arline McCubbin on one of our special visits, she remembered the atmosphere of Alberta's Tea Room was warm and inviting.

"The food was wonderful, and the décor was beautiful. Ms. McCubbin also stated that the Tea Room was "THE PLACE" to go for a special event. She let me know that Alberta's Tea Room made a lot of people happy."
-Ms. D'Arline McCubbin

"I remember that Grandma did not play when it came to my brother LP. She pulled out her checkbook. She had $97.00 cash and was going to write a check for the balance due. I thought $100.00 was too much if you ask me."

-Jacqueline Ponder Dyson

"I guess I first met Alberta at the Tea Room. I feel like I met her at a family gathering before that but I'm not sure. I know my mom and aunts and their friends loved to go there. I had a wedding shower there, a baby shower and then went to a study group at French Market mall. After our children were born Easter Brunch there was a favorite too. My favorite dish – Chicken Salad! Or wait could have been the rolls or the green beans or the tarts! Everything was delicious and the Beef Tenderloins cannot be beat.

I also remember having the Glenbrook neighborhood Christmas parties there - all dressed up.

It was so fun and so many of us still talk about it and how we miss it. It was a one-of-a-kind place, to gather and enjoy delicious food."
-Mrs. Betsy Thorpe

"My favorite memory of my grandmother and The Alberta's Tea Room is going to work there when I was a young girl. I remember the day the Civil Rights Activist Rosa Parks came for a Luncheon as the guest speaker for the National Forum for Black Public

Administrators Sooner Chapter. That was an amazing day I will never forget.

I enjoyed going to the Tearoom, especially to eat all the different homemade dishes my grandparents would cook. We were blessed to be able to work and have our own money at the age of 12/13 years old when our friends were not.

My other memory is always knowing my grandmother and Anee would always pray in the morning, all through the day and night! That is where we found that everything happens after prayer and always pray and put God first. "

-Deanna Williams

Alberta's Tea Room and the Dessert Table on Mother's Day

Alberta and James with 50th
Wedding Anniversary Cake

James Brannon with his sons

Sons with wives and family friend Graciel King

James and Alberta in kitchen at French Market Mall

Alberta plating Neiman Marcus Bars

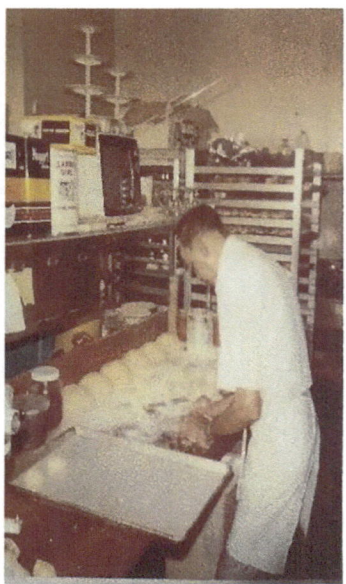

Bakery Chef, James Brannon,
rolling out loaf bread

Elicia Brannon, serving at fruit and cheese table

Chef Larry Brannon, building a fruit pyramid

PART V

"THE CLOSING OF ALBERTA'S TEA ROOM"

"LET THE WORDS OF MY MOUTH AND THE MEDITATION OF MY HEART, BE ACCEPTABLE IN THY SIGHT, O LORD, MY STRENGTH, AND MY REDEEMER."

PSALM 19:14

Alberta's Tea Room was the place to go for an elegant affair, large or small, for nearly thirty years. However, Roy Lee Brannon, the manager, tried to keep the business afloat. After the matriarch was no longer able to carry the restaurant part of the business forward, it was decided in April 1998 to close the restaurant permanently. However, Chef James Jr. and Chef Larry continued the catering business, serving their clients in their homes and other private venues throughout Oklahoma City and surrounding areas.

Sadly, on April 28, 2008, ten years after the closing of the Tea Room, Alberta Brannon closed her eyes on this earth to open them in Heaven, resting in the arms of her Lord and Savior Jesus Christ.

The Oklahoma City Community Foundation, along with the Brannon family, started a scholarship fund in honor of our "MOM" and "Grandmother" Alberta Brannon, to give a helping hand to young people interested in the culinary arts program. To date, several awards have been shared through the Alberta Brannon Memorial Scholarship.

In February 2009, our family said goodbye to our beloved A-nee, Ethel Susong, who went to Heaven to receive her crown and be with the Lord. Seven months after Aunt Ethel passed, to our shock, Roy Lee Brannon, the second son of James and Alberta, passed away in September 2009 as well.

We cherish the memories of our loving Mother, Father, Aunt, and brothers that are resting. We will never forget the impact that they had on our lives.

The Oklahoma History Center asked the Brannon family if they would mind sharing the story of Alberta's Tea Room with the world in a display at the History Center. With great pride and excitement, the Brannon family gladly agreed to share the original menus from the restaurant, the Channel 5 interview with B.J. Glover and Anthony Foster, and a live interview with Chef James Jr., Executive Catering Chef Larry, and their sister Darlene Reed. The display was opened to the public in May 2015 and remains open today.

———————————————————

I always looked forward to enjoying an elegant dining experience on Mother's Day at the "Tea Room." The atmosphere was always first class and the service was excellent. I loved bringing my mother there as my gift to her, and she looked forward to it as well.

What stands out in my mind, as I look back, was the beautiful atmosphere. Everything was bright and very clean. The white tablecloths gave you the feeling that they were not just another restaurant. Of course I loved the wonderful, tasty food. My favorite was baked chicken, but there was a variety of entrees that were equally cooked to perfection. The veggies were very tasty and seasoned well, but not over seasoned. Now the Rolls, were in a class of its own and was another favorite. I had to remind myself to behave and not over-eat those "melt-in your mouth rolls."

"Another thing that stood out to me was how the desserts were displayed at the Mother's Day dinner. It allowed us freedom to see them up close and choose and the decision was tough. I wanted everything. Now I must point out that the apple pie with rum sauce was my favorite dessert."-

"When I think of the "Tea Room" what comes to mind is: Excellence of service, excellence of food, and family. I still miss "Alberta's Tea Room." It was a place where we enjoyed weddings, receptions, banquets and of course Mother's Day Dinner."

-Bernae Richardson

"I remember when Grandma offered Lonnie and I $100.00 for LP. We said "SURE!" She started digging in her purse. I was like "grandma, it was a joke". She looked up with a not so happy look. She always favored the boys."

-Mrs. Marvinette Ponder

"My best memories of Alberta's Tea Room were coming to work in the morning and smelling the aroma of fresh baked rolls and apple pies that Pop Brannon was creating. That would set the mood in the morning in the right direction. The first person you would see, would be Alberta Brannon, cutting up fresh fruit, she would greet you with a smile and call you young(en). She would always save me the cores of the pineapple she had been cutting early that morning and sometime have a small cup of grapefruit slices waiting for me. After our hellos, I would sneak my way over to where the freshly baked rolls, loaf bread, buns, and pies were on the cooling racks and abscond with two or three rolls before the watchful eye of Pop's would spot me."

"Probably the best thing about the Tea Room was everything made fresh from freshly cut fruit to homemade bread and soups. All the food and gravy and sauces were made from scratch. Alberta would make me make her fruit dressing which I hated to do and make the famous Rum sauce, things I did not appreciate then, but boy I do now! Once someone said to me Reggie can you cook, and my mind race back to the days of the Tea Room and Alberta herself and I would say "Yes" I sure can!"

-Reggie Littlejohn

"As a child I say around 5 or 6 years old me and grandma had a special bond. Now you might ask why your bond was so special, glad you asked. Being the first grandchild and a girl!! What were those odds? Well do I need to say any more? Grandma Burt always knew when I was having a not so good day. She would show up

we would have a girl talk and to make it a sweet talk grandma would look in her purse and pull out a pack of Wrigley's juicy fruit gum you know the kind in the yellow package wrapped in silver paper. She always made my day when she let me have a stick of gum, it was so good. I forgot how bad my day was going. That was just one of the most memorable days of my grandma Burt. I miss grandma and I will never forget her, she was one of a kind.

-Debbie Horton

"I have many fond memories of Grandma Bert. That's what we kids called her. My dad's mother; she was always on the move. I don't think she stopped much or stayed in one spot for too long.

Grandma Bert did a lot of things and most everyone knew her as Alberta, the cook. She was better than just any cook; she was certainly so much more.

My Grandmother had, over fifty grandchildren and great-grand children back in the 80's. I remember our family celebrating my Grandparents' Fiftieth Wedding Anniversary when I was in the fourth grade, and my mom and aunts spent an amount of time naming and counting all my cousins and their children. All I knew was it was a lot of us!

My mother used to babysit for family members, so my cousins would often come over to our house. On a few occasions Grandma Bert would let my mom drive her LTD station wagon by Ford. It had the regular back seat and then another fold up seat in the very back. My Mom would load it full of Brannon cousins and off to the park we would go. Stars and Stripes Park or Memorial Park at 36th and Western and sometimes we would go to Dolphin Park right up the street from Grandma's House. There was also a park across the street from the Tea Room at

French Market Mall that had a play area and a swimming pool and we loved going there as well.

Grandma Bert's house was at the bottom of the hill on 63 rd. Street between Kelley Ave. and Broadway Extension. The house is still there, with the orange front door. We would go to Grandma and Grandpa's house all the time. As a child it seemed like every week. Grandpa would cook and everybody (All my uncles, aunts, and cousins) would go over on Sunday after church and eat. I still miss Grandpa's fried chicken, okra, greens, and creamed corn. He made a special cornbread and a chocolate delight; however, I believe the family favorite was his peach cobbler. Lord have mercy! I was a child, but I still remember my grandpa's cooking. Though my dad comes very close, no one has matched his peach cobbler. My, my, my, good, good, good, good, good.

After we ate the kids would all go back to Grandma and Grandpa's bedroom and watch T.V. or we would go outside and play. They had a big iron swing set that we would play on. The house had a creek that ran right next to it. My brothers and some of my cousins would go down in it and play around, but I was too scared to go down there and so I just stuck to playing in the yard and on the swing set.

Grandma Bert's house always had special visitors - peacocks. Yes, peacocks. Who in the world has peacocks coming by to visit daily? Grandma Bert did. Sometimes just one, other times several would be seen walking around in her driveway like they lived there. I loved to see them spread their wings and show their glorious colors.

Grandma Bert led a Morning Prayer at our church, Monday through Saturday from 6:00

a.m. to 7:00 a.m. She and a group of other ladies and gentlemen would pray for the special needs of people as well all for their community. Dad said that a man who was a boxer would come and join in the prayer. The group would pray for each other and ask God to heal people. They prayed for miracles. God performed many, including healing my sixteen-year-old brother of cancer.

When she would get ready to end each prayer session, she daily would say, "Lord, we thank you for preserving our homes and the homes of people everywhere", she would also say, "Lord keep speaking to us through your word."

She worked for some of the wealthiest families in Oklahoma, but I saw her treat the poor with the same love and respect as everyone else. I do not think she ever met a stranger. Around her, everyone was family or a friend.

I enjoyed sitting with Grandma at church on Sundays. In her Bible she had pictures of some of my family members that I never tired of viewing, but one Sunday I was not excited to sit with Grandma. My parents had gone out of town and my brothers and I were staying with our cousins. I was looking forward to getting a break and not going to church on that Sunday, but Grandma would have none of that, she called and told us to all get ready. She came by and picked up my brothers, my cousins and me in her station wagon and took us all to church.

At the Tea Room as we called it, I loved to sit on a stool in Grandma's area and just sit and watch her. I loved to watch her prepare the grapefruit for the fruit cups and fruit plates. First, she would peel the grapefruit, then she would slice each section of the grapefruit with a knife. I was mesmerized at how quickly and precise she did this without cutting herself. I also was amazed to watch her make her homemade fruit salad dressing. I never acquired the taste for what so many people raved over, yet I loved watching her make it. I could not wrap my mind around the fact that something she was preparing to place on fruit has onion as one of the ingredients.

Grandma Bert would move around the kitchen at ease. She did not have a problem running the dishwasher or sweeping the floor. She did everything with a whistle. It was fun to me to watch her operate the cash register and make change for customers as well as see her make plates for a large ladies' luncheon or some church banquet. When Grandma was not busy, she and Mrs. Jean (Mrs. Erma Jean also a Morning Prayer Member and employee over the soup and salad station) would make quilts. She would clean her station up and lay out her quilt squares right there on her work table. I am not sure how many quilts they made over the years, but I believe it is more that can be counted. I have one on my bed right now.

-Carla D. Brannon

"One of my fondest childhood memories of Grandma Bert is participating in early morning prayer with her at Page Sanctuary Church of God in Christ, located on 2nd & Byers Street in Oklahoma City. My mom would wake me up, letting me know it was time to get ready because my grandmother was heading to our house to pick me up for early morning prayer. Sometimes, it would be dark and cold outside, and she would be wrapped up in her coat or shawl.

Grandma Bert owned a peach color station wagon. Her sister, Ethel Susong, affectionately known as Nanny, would always ride in the front seat. After picking me up at our Forest Park home, her journey began by picking up some of the members of her prayer team, which included Mother Vincent, Sister Cordelia, and Mother Hill. Once all the ladies were picked up, we headed to the church.

The streets were so peaceful then, almost sacred in their silence. Once we got to the church, I was sometimes afraid to get out of grandma's car. In previous years before Urban Renewal, the area of the church was not in the best location. Sometimes, there would be night walkers hanging around in the area, which frightened me. It never seemed to bother the Prayer Warrior team. Once they were in the church, they would lock the door, and prayer time began.

Their prayers were so powerful that it felt like the room moved. This would go on for a few hours, and they prayed with such conviction, every word filled with love, gratitude, and deep faith. I did not always understand every word of the prayers, but I understood how serious they were about seeking God early in the morning. Those mornings were not just rituals, they were sacred moments where I learned to talk to God, not out of obligation, but out of relationship. I saw in her a faith that was alive, intimate, and unshakable. It was there, by their side, that the seeds of my faith were planted. These ladies were the epitome of James 5:16, which states that the "fervent effectual prayer of a righteous man availeth much." They were truly dedicated and committed to this task. Later, I learned that my grandmother did this for 30-plus years.

In addition to accompanying my grandmother to early morning prayer, once I decided to attend an "all night" prayer vigil. My eyes grew tired and sleepy, and I fell asleep on the pew. Mother Vincent woke me up and stated, "Baby, you must stay awake. It's time to pray." Well, I guess that's what they meant about "All Night Prayer."

Today, whenever I pray, I often think about hearing my mom and grandmother praying in the Spirit. Their devotion became the foundation of my relationship with God. That quiet time of prayer, so simple yet so powerful, remains the pillar of my faith – a constant reminder of where I came from and who guides me still."

-Barbara Brannon-King

James, Bobby Ray and
Alberta Brannon

Harold Brannon with his mother Alberta

Ethel Susong, Alberta's sister

Alberta and granddaughter, Carla Brannon

Alberta, Ethel, Johnsie Carter and Barbara
on Mother's Day

Alberta's Tea Room Manager,
Roy Lee Brannon

PART VI

"THE LEGACY OF ALBERTA SUSONG-BRANNON & JAMES L. BRANNON"

Married March 21, 1936

(The number in front of each name represents the generation they are in)

1-Alberta Brannon + James L. Brannon
2-James Brannon + Mary E. Clark-Brannon

3-Debbie L. Brannon-Horton +Marshall Horton

4-Marshall Otis L. Horton +Ayana Horton

5-Mia Horton

5-Marshall Ty

5-Jillian Horton

4-Ashyle D. Horton

4-Ariel L. Horton-Jones +Jimel Jones

5-Austin Jones

5-Steven Jones

3-Delbert L. Brannon

4-Joab D. Golson

4-Mesha Brannon

5-Antonio Brannon

5-Myesha Brannon

5-DeMarko Brannon

4-Montia Brannon

5-Tiana Brannon

5-Deana Brannon

5-Jeremiah Brannon

5-Monty Brannon

5-Magic Brannon

4-Darlecia Brannon

5-Analicia Brannon

4-Justin Brannon

3-Deneese L. Brannon-Long + Michael Long
4-Prentice Hunt, Jr. + ShaRandia Hunt
5-PraSiah Hunt
5-Prenceton Hunt
4-Rickey T.L. Hunt + Darise Hunt
5-Rickey T. L. Hunt, Jr.
5-Rickel Hunt
5-Darius Hunt
4-Jamil D. Hunt + Eliza Hunt
5-Ja'Nea D Hunt
5-Jamil D. Hunt, Jr.
5-Jru P. Hunt
5-Jade L. Hunt
5-E'Lexius Taylor
5-Ahrye E. Taylor
4-Denard W. C. Hunt + LaTrelda Hunt
5-Kalub J. Hunt
5-Payton L. Hunt
5-Mae R. Hunt
5-Denard W. C. Hunt, Jr.
3-Darren Brannon
4-Darren Brannon, Jr.
5-Darren Brannon III
3-Doshon Brannon-Williams + Lester Williams
4-Otis Thompson, Jr. + Ronesha Thompson
5-Otis Thompson III
5-Olijah Thompson
4-Olivia N. Flores + Josue Flores

5-Eva Flores

5-Roman Flores

4-Omar Thompson

4-Jeremiah Thompson

3-James L. Brannon IV + Shayla Brannon

2-<u>Roy Lee Brannon Sr + Hattie Broadnax-Brannon</u>

3-Antoinette Brannon-Carruthers + Daryl Carruthers, Sr.

4-Daryl C. Carruthers, Jr.

4-Daryn A. Carruthers + Tonya J. Carruthers

5-Daryn Carruthers II

5-Mia Carruthers

5-Micah A. Carruthers

4-Damon B. Carruthers + Neteshia T. Carruthers

5-Christopher B. Carruthers

3-Roy Lee Brannon, Jr.

4-Christina M. Brannon-Pierce + Douglas L. Pierce

5-Bryce L. Pierce

5-Maia M. Pierce

3-Byron K. Brannon

3-Steven F. Brannon

2-<u>Bobby Ray Brannon Sr + Wilma Baldwin-Brannon</u>

3-Barbara R. Brannon-King + Michael King

4-Royal S. Brannon

4-Marcus King + Kassidy King

5-Kashen King

5-Kaelyn King

5-Kruz King

3-DeAnna Brannon-Williams + John Williams

4-LaQuoia R. Jones + Rickey Jones, Jr.

5-Rickey Jones III

5-Brayln Jones

5-Brooklyn Jones

4-John H. Williams III + Samaya Williams

5-Ja'ell Williams

4-Bobby R. Williams, Sr. + Brittany Williams

5-Bobby R. Williams, Jr.

5-Levi Williams

5-Anderson Williams

3-Bobby Ray Brannon, Jr.

4-Shavon Brannon

4-Sharai Brannon-Johnson + Cedric Johnson

5-Serenity Johnson

5-Julian Johnson

4-Khyree Brannon

5-Savannah Brannon

5-Amari Brannon

3-Mary Brannon-Jackson + Larry Jackson

4-Isaiah Brannon

3-Dion Brannon

2-Marvin Eugene Brannon, Sr. + Charlene Meeks-Brannon

3-Marvinette J. Brannon-Ponder + Alonzo L. Ponder II

4-Jocquelene F. Ponder-Dyson + DaShaven Dyson, Jr.

5-Natalya J. Dyson

5-DaShaven D. Dyson III

5-Paris E. Dyson

5-Aiden G. Dyson

4-Alonzo L. Ponder III

5-Alonzo L. Ponder IV.

3-Elicia Brannon-Little

4-Jiovoni E. Brannon + Ashley Brannon

5-Elicia D. Brannon

4-Jade A. Little

4-Haylie L. Little-Calicott + Darnell Calicott

5-Isabella E. Calicott

3-Marvin E. Brannon, Jr.

4-Sada L. Brannon

4-Charlene D. Brannon

5-Nailata Day

4-Drelon R. Brannon

3-Teffany I. Brannon

4-Charles H. Brannon

5-Amiyah Brannon

5-Kamden Brannon

5-Ian Brannon

4-Toni A. Brannon-Johnson + Brandon Johnson, Sr.

5-Brandon Johnson, Jr.

5-Bralen Johnson

3-Mary R. Brannon

2-Alberta Darlene Brannon + Don V. Reed

3-Kenneth Robinson + Jessica Robinson

4-Karlos Robinson

5-Kiana Robinson

4-Kendall Robinson

3-Dawn Williams

4-Joshlyn Johnson

4-Darralyn Williams-Reed + Aaron Reed

5-Fall Reed

5-Noah Reed

5-Ezra Reed

5-Chloe Reed

4-Jordan Williams

3-Dehrone Mack

4-Kalah Harding

4-Isaiah Wilcots + Emily Wilcots

5-Ivy Wilcots

2-Harold Lynn Brannon, Sr. + Karlette George-Brannon

3-Harold L. Brannon, Jr. + Susan Brannon

4-Ibrahim Brannon

4-Iman Brannon

3-Scott H. Brannon + Emily Brannon

4-Gabriel Brannon

4-Lillian Brannon

3-Alberta K. Brannon-Hackett + Corey Hackett

4-Kori Hackett

4-Rian Hackett

4-Nicholas Hackett

3-Garvice M. Brannon

3-Barbara Brannon

2-Larry Franklin Brannon Sr. + Barbara J. Duff-Brannon

3-Larry F. Brannon II + Jena Payne-Brannon
4-Michelle J. Brannon
4-Kolin J. Brannon
4-Nathan S. Brannon
3-David L. Brannon + LaWanda M. Woods-Brannon
4-Kayla N. Brannon
4-Jillian R. Brannon
4-Jackson L. Brannon
3-Carla D. Brannon

"WRITE THE VISION, AND MAKE IT PLAIN UPON TABLES, THAT HE MAY RUN THAT READETH IT."
HABAKKUK 2:2

After I published my first book, ONE LIFE, MANY TESTIMONIES: A LEGACY OF GOD'S GRACE AND MERCY, I began to hear "there is another book in you." I could not get the thought out of my mind. Then I was asked by a few people when the next book was coming out. The vision began to come clear; to write the story of The Alberta Brannon. I started my research and making notes. With the help of my family and friends, my project has come a long way in just a few years. I truly loved my Mother-In-Law: She meant so much to me. A virtuous woman that I looked up to with love, respect, and honor. She was a great influence in teaching me as I watched her live a holy life, be a godly daughter, wife, mother, sister, and friend. I am truly grateful and blessed to be a part of this amazing family.

Barbara Duff-Brannon